Copyright © 2019, Katriel Tolin.

All rights reserved. This book or parts thereof may not be reproduced in any form, stored in any retrieval system, or transmitted in any form by any means—electronic, mechanical, photocopy, recording, or otherwise—without prior written permission of the publisher, except as provided by United States of America copyright law. Send permission requests to author.

ISBN: 978-0-578-52368-2 (Paperback)

ACKNOWLEDGMENTS

I would like to thank Ms. Minwalla, Dr. Larson, and Ms. Kendall for supporting me throughout this endeavor. Each of you brought a wealth of knowledge that guided me and made this process enjoyable. I would also like to thank Dr. Maureen Graham for her dedication to this project, and for offering me direction when it was necessary. Thank you to my parents for always listening and learning with me. To Trinity, you were my motivation behind this cathartic labor of love—thank you.

TABLE OF CONTENTS

Introduction

Chapter 1: What are anxiety and depression?

Chapter 2: Why is there a stigma?

Chapter 3: Mental Health & the African American Community

Chapter 4: How to Cope

Chapter 5: But My Parents Don't Understand!

Chapter 6: Highs + Lows

INTRODUCTION

I feel I should begin by saying that I am in no way an expert in most of the stuff in this book. I'm simply an 18-year-old (I began this project when I was 17!) who has gone through some pretty difficult stuff and really felt like there needed to be a resource out there for kids who may experience the same stuff I did. I found it difficult to reach out for help when I felt incredibly misunderstood, when I was in middle school I didn't have anything like this to help me when I needed it most. So, I decided that I would make it myself! I believe that this book could become a medium for kiddos to find understanding.

I did the research and read all of the long articles so that you guys, the readers, wouldn't have to. I wanted anyone who needed this information to be able to easily access it without shame, embarrassment, or the feeling that someone may not understand. I was drawn to this topic because at some point I thought no one understood me, and now I want to tell everyone that it does get better (ugh, I know). I hope you enjoy this thing I have created, and I hope it can help you. This book is for everyone to learn a bit about themselves and others. And to remind you that when it feels like no one cares or understands--I do.

KATRIEL

Chapter 1

What are ANXIETY and DEPRESSION?

*definition provided by Dr. Maureen Graham

DEFINITION: A MOOD DISORDER THAT NEGATIVELY AFFECTS INDIVIDUALS FEELINGS, THE WAY THEY THINK, AND HOW THEY ACT. INDIVIDUALS EXPERIENCING DEPRESSION HAVE PERSISTENT FEELING OF SADNESS AND EXHIBIT LOSS OF INTEREST IN ACTIVITIES THAT THEY PREVIOUSLY ENJOYED.*

SYMPTOMS

- Feelings of sadness, tearfulness, emptiness or hopelessness
- Angry outbursts, irritability or frustration, even over small matters
- Loss of interest or pleasure in most or all normal activities, such as hobbies or sports
- Sleep disturbances, including insomnia or sleeping too much
- Tiredness and lack of energy, so even small tasks take extra effort
- Reduced appetite and weight loss or increased cravings for food and weight gain
- Anxiety, agitation or restlessness
- Slowed thinking, speaking or body movements
- Feelings of worthlessness or guilt, fixating on past failures or self-blame
- Trouble thinking, concentrating, making decisions and remembering things

*definition provided by Dr. Maureen Graham

DEFINITION: A NERVOUS DISORDER WITH INDICATIONS OF EXCESSIVE UNEASINESS AND APPREHENSION, WITH INDIVIDUALS SOMETIMES EXHIBITING COMPULSIVE BEHAVIOR OR PANIC ATTACKS.*

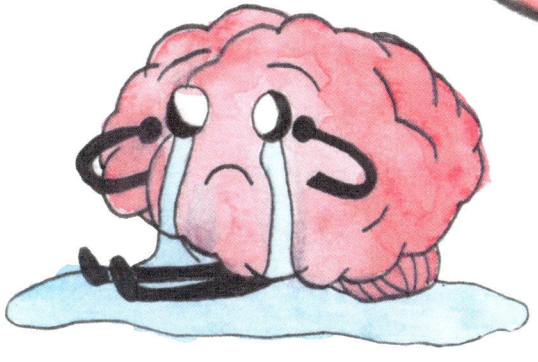

SYMPTOMS

- Feeling nervous, restless or tense
- Having a sense of impending danger, panic or doom
- Having an increased heart rate
- Breathing rapidly (hyperventilation)
- Sweating
- Trembling
- Feeling weak or tired
- Trouble concentrating or thinking about anything other than the present worry
- Having trouble sleeping
- Experiencing gastrointestinal (GI) problems
- Having difficulty controlling worry
- Having the urge to avoid things that trigger anxiety

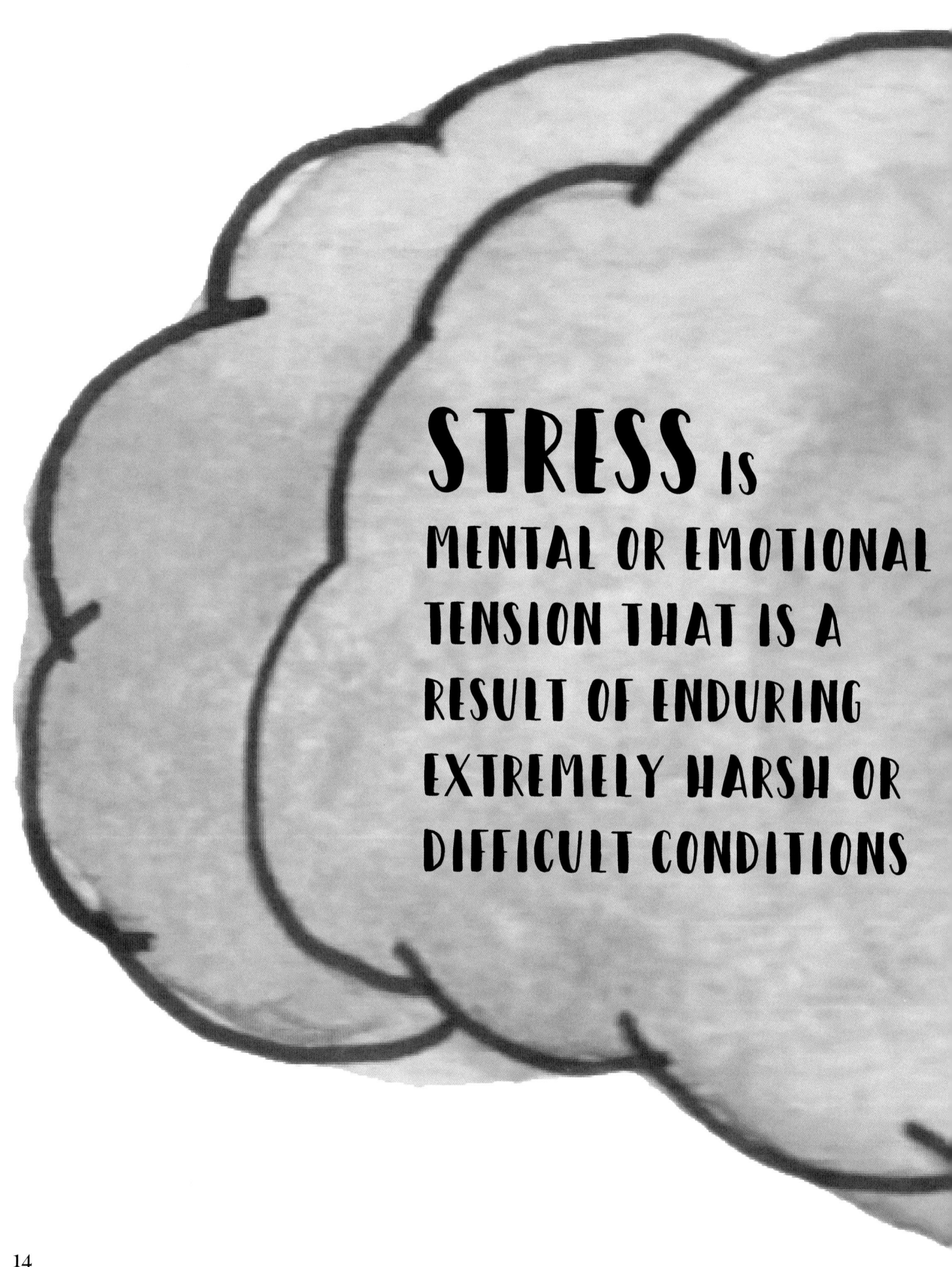

STRESS is mental or emotional tension that is a result of enduring extremely harsh or difficult conditions

*definition provided by Dr. Maureen Graham

TRAUMA IS THE RESPONSE TO A VERY DISTRESSING OR TROUBLING EVENT THAT CONTRIBUTES TO AN INDIVIDUALS INABILITY TO ADEQUATELY COPE, THUS LEADING TO FEELINGS OF HELPLESSNESS, A LESSENING SENSE OF SELF, AND INABILITY TO FEEL THE FULL RANGE OF EMOTIONS AND EXPERIENCES.*

Chapter 2

Why is there a stigma?

HOW IS IT DEVELOPED?

Stigma is developed mainly by misinformation and a lack of understanding. When large groups of people support preconceived notions that create a false negative view, that is a stigma.

WHAT ARE THE EFFECTS OF STIGMA?

Stigma may prevent someone from seeking help due to fear of being scrutinized or considered crazy. It may also cause an individual to deny the severity of their mental health issues. This is dangerous in that it aggravates the symptoms of anxiety and depression.

WHAT CAN I DO?

Reducing the effects of stigma is the first step to developing a healthy approach to mental health issues. It begins by starting conversations about anxiety and depression, and by having an appropriate response when you or someone else seeks out help.

Read the comics on the next page to see how positive conversations about mental health can alleviate stigma.

A BAD EXCHANGE

A PROPER EXCHANGE

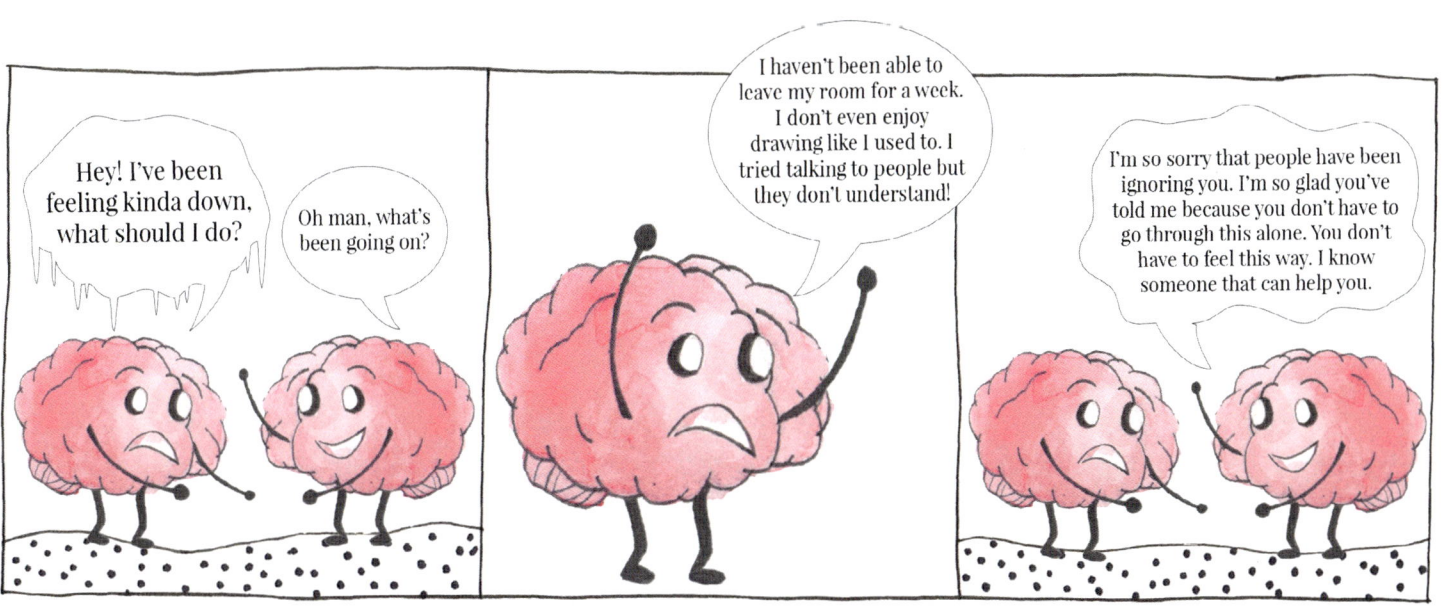

DON'T LET STIGMA BE A BURDEN!

While it is difficult to ignore what others are telling you, it is important for your mental wellbeing to remember that no one else can tell you how you feel. If you feel like no one is taking your concerns seriously--whether it be a friend, teacher, sibling or parent--you must prioritize your mental health yourself. It is not your job to teach everyone else how to understand you, especially when you are under extreme stress. There are resources specifically meant to help you get the information you need (like this). So, don't let other's ignorance discourage you. Your emotions are real and valid.

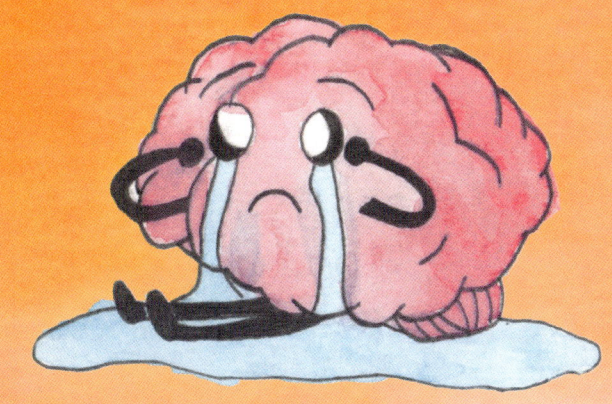

Chapter 3

Mental Health & the African American Community

THE COMMUNITY'S APPROACH TO MENTAL HEALTH

Mental health has only recently become a socially accepted discussion topic; even further, it has not become a culturally accepted subject in the African American community. Most of this generation's parents or caregivers grew up in a society where focusing on the importance of mental health was not a priority. Sometimes when a kid reveals a mental struggle to their parents, the kid may receive a dismissive reply. It is often difficult for adults to adapt to newly accepted ideas that reject what they have always known.

This is especially true in the African American community. African Americans often grew up being told to be strong, so this teaching is applied to their own children. Historically, African Americans have overcome major obstacles such as slavery, racism, and high poverty rates. Throughout all of the turmoil, we have depicted ourselves as people of unwavering strength. Thus, we have made it culturally dishonorable to have mental illnesses due to our inability to be emotionally vulnerable or fragile in public. As an African American woman, I understand how damaging and unrealistic tropes such as "strong, independent black woman" can be to emotional development. I feel it is important for us to recognize the damage that this mindset is for us as a community and its members individually.

COMMUNITY

Only 30% of African Americans seek medical treatment (v. 63% national average).

Over 18.6% of African Americans have a diagnosable mental illness.

1 in 3 African Americans who need mental health services receive it.

Black teens are more likely to attempt suicide than white teens.

STATISTICS

Physicians are 33% less engaged in patient-centered communication with African American patients than white patients.

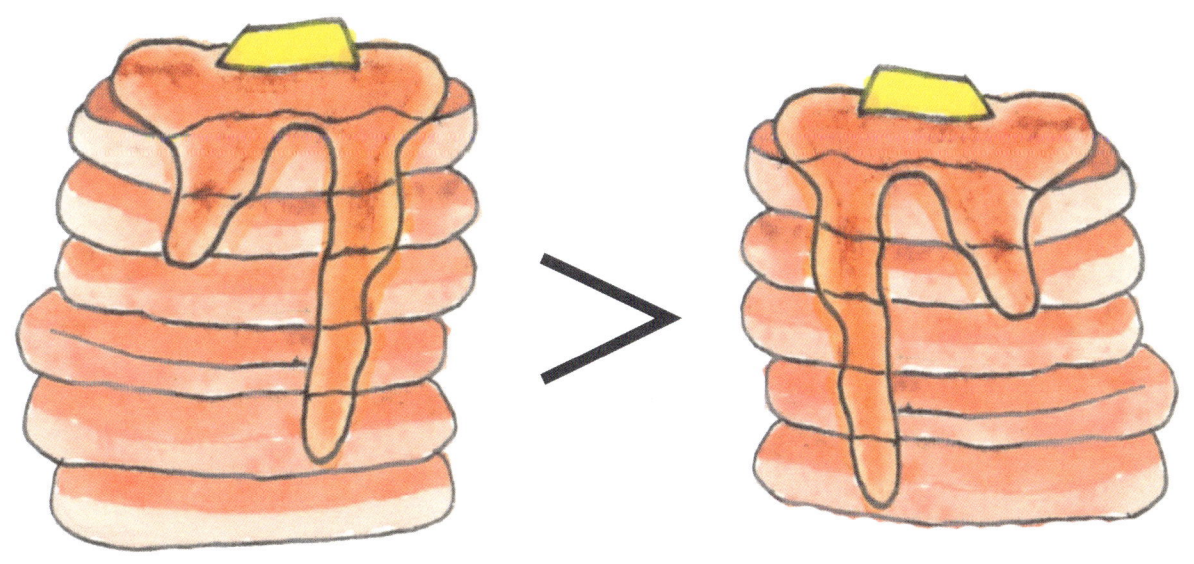

African Americans adults are 20% more likely to experience psychological distress than white people.

COMMUNITY ALTOGETHER

Statistics prove that African Americans do not properly handle or prioritize their mental health. As a community, we must acknowledge the danger of our negligence.

This begins by having open conversations with members of our community about the importance of mental health awareness. If you notice someone is suffering in silence--talk to them. If a person is spreading false information or shaming someone for speaking up about their mental health issues--correct them. The more informed we become as a community, the easier it will be for individuals to receive the care they need.

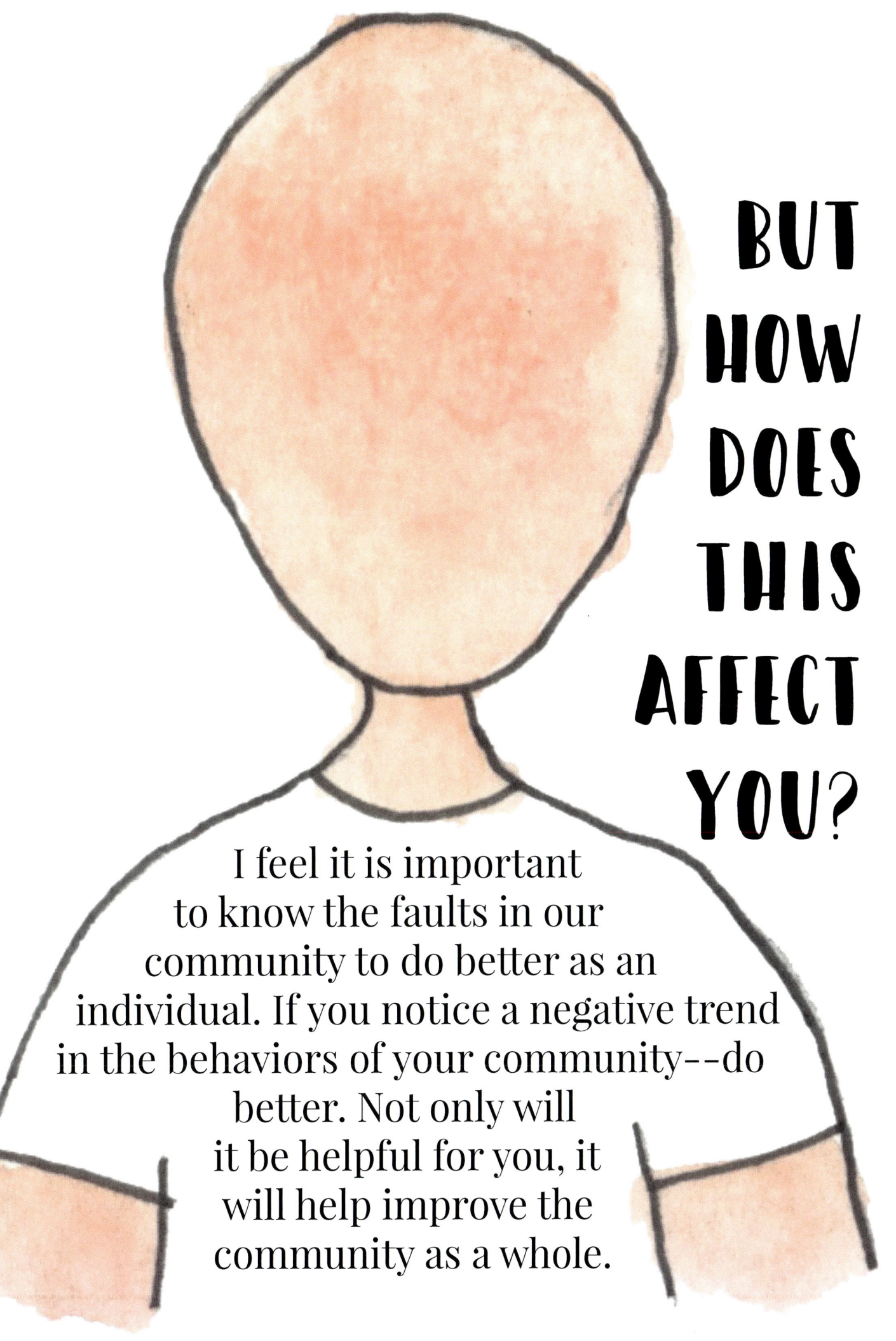

SOME BADGES FOR YOU!

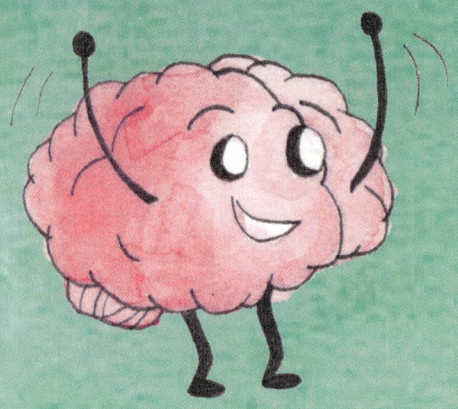

Chapter 4

How to Cope

WHAT ARE THE DIFFERENT FORMS OF COPING?

- solving the problem
- non-productive coping
- reference to others

These three coping categories form the Adolescent Coping Scale. This helps us understand what coping behaviors are appropriate in certain situations. Having an idea of the variety of coping methods that are available can help you determine what works best for you!

The Adolescent Coping Scale

WHAT IS THE ADOLESCENT COPING SCALE?
THE DIFFERENT METHODS USED BY TEENS TO COPE WITH STRESS. SOME OF THE METHODS PROVE TO BE HELPFUL WHILE OTHERS ARE HARMFUL.

1) SEEK SOCIAL SUPPORT: THE PROCESS OF SHARING A PROBLEM OR STRESSOR WITH ANOTHER PERSON IN ORDER TO RECEIVE HELP AND SUPPORT

2) FOCUS ON SOLVING THE PROBLEM: A VIEW THAT FOCUSES ON LEARNING EVERY ASPECT OF THE PROBLEM AND USING THE INFORMATION LEARNED TO ADDRESS THE STRESSOR IN A STRATEGIC WAY

3) WORK HARD AND ACHIEVE: AN AMBITIOUS APPROACH THAT PRIORITIZES WORKING HARD TO REACH CERTAIN GOALS OR PERFORM GENERALLY WELL

4) WORRY: ANXIETY! EXTREME CONCERN ABOUT WHAT IS HAPPENING NOW AND THE PROSPECTS OF ONE'S FUTURE, OFTEN FIXATED ON THE BELIEF THAT ONE MAY NOT BE HAPPY IN THE FUTURE

5) SEEK TO BELONG: CONCERN ABOUT THE STATE OF ONE'S RELATIONSHIPS AND CARING ABOUT WHAT OTHERS THINK TO THE POINT OF WORRY

6) INVEST IN CLOSE FRIENDS: DEPENDENCE ON A PARTICULARLY IMPORTANT AND CLOSE RELATIONSHIP, WHETHER IT A ROMANTIC OR PLATONIC RELATIONSHIP

7) SOCIAL ACTION: THE SPREADING OF INFORMATION TO A LARGE AUDIENCE WITH THE HOPES OF GETTING A SUPPORTIVE COMMUNITY TOGETHER AND ORGANIZING EVENTS, ESPECIALLY THROUGH THE MEANS OF SOCIAL MEDIA

8) TENSION REDUCTION: THE USE OF ITEMS IN AN ATTEMPT TO RELIEVE TENSION OR STRESS, USUALLY TAKES THE FORM OF SUBSTANCE ABUSE

9) SEEK SPIRITUAL SUPPORT: TURNING TO RELIGION, CHURCH, OR ANY OTHER SPIRITUAL BELIEF TO SEEK GUIDANCE OR RELIEF

10) **SEEK RELAXING DIVERSIONS:** TO TAKE PART IN LEISURE ACTIVITIES THAT OFFER RELAXING QUALITIES

11) **IGNORE THE PROBLEM:** THE ACCEPTANCE OF THE BELIEF THAT THERE IS NO WAY TO HANDLE THE PROBLEM, THUS ONE MAY NOT ADDRESS THE PROBLEM ALTOGETHER

12) **NOT COPE:** THE DECISION TO NOT DEAL WITH THE PROBLEM, BUT RATHER DEAL WITH THE CONSEQUENCES OF THE PROBLEM

13) **KEEP TO SELF:** PULLING AWAY FROM THE PEOPLE IN ONE'S LIFE TO KEEP PEOPLE FROM KNOWING HOW ONE FEELS

14) **WISHFUL THINKING:** THE PROCESS OF HOPING THINGS WILL END POSITIVELY AND MAINTAINING AN OPTIMISTIC OUTLOOK

15) **SELF-BLAME:** WHEN ONE CONSIDERS THEMSELVES SOLELY RESPONSIBLE FOR ONE'S PROBLEM; A NEGATIVE PERSPECTIVE THAT PUTS THE AFFECTED PERSON AT FAULT

16) **PHYSICAL RECREATION:** PARTICIPATION IN SPORTS OR OTHER ATHLETIC ACTIVITIES TO STAY HEALTHY

17) **FOCUS ON THE POSITIVE:** TO REMAIN POSITIVE DURING THE SITUATION ONE IS IN AND FOCUS ON THE GOOD IN ONE'S LIFE

COPING SKILLS IN ACTION

Now that you have a knowledge of what coping is and some of the coping methods that you may use, it is important that you distinguish the positive coping skills from the negative ones. For instance:

worry, wishful thinking, tension reduction, not cope, ignore the problem, self-blame, and keep to self < seek social support, focus on solving the problem, work hard and achieve, invest in close friends, seek to belong, focus on the positive, seek relaxing diversions, and physical recreation, social action, seek social support, seek spiritual support, and seek professional help

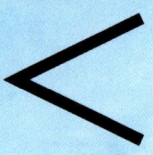

Not all coping skills have to be intentional. Healthy coping can take place in the form of self-care habits such as getting out of bed when you don't feel like it, doing your homework Friday night so that you have a free weekend, or staying in with your friends to watch a movie. I like to listen to music and dance in my bedroom to blow off steam.

HOW RELIGION CAN BE HELPFUL

Whether you practice religion on your own or with your family, religion can often be a positive force in our lives. It can provide guidance and comfort through difficult times. If you already have a strong religious background, your relationship with God can provide and optimistic view of your situation.

If possible, reach out to smaller groups within your church to create a community that you can share your experiences with. If you choose to use religious coping methods, it is important to focus on healthy methods that will make your relieve your stress rather than worsen it.

A few helpful religious coping mechanisms:
- Believing that you can solve the problem through a partnership with God.
- Seeking support from members of your church or leaders in your church.
- Using your belief to forgive yourself and release any negative feelings associated with the stressor.
- Leaning on God for a sense of love and comfort.

HOW RELIGION CAN BE HARMFUL

For those who do not practice religion on a regular basis or have a tumultuous relationship with God or any other religious figure, religion often has a negative effect on one's mental state. It can cause reliance on harmful religious coping mechanisms that worsen the symptoms of a stressor and prompt self-blame.

A few harmful religious coping mechanisms:
- Believing that a stressor or difficult situation is a punishment from God.
- Believing that simply through prayer and devotion the stressor will go away.
- Waiting for God to solve the problem for you.

If you are under pressure from your parents or people in your life to use religious coping methods, be open about how that may make you uncomfortable. Often, deeply religious people invalidate the seriousness of mental health as a whole. It is important to find a balance between prioritizing your relationship with your religion and spending time on your mental health.

Chapter 5

But my parents don't understand!

A MAJOR DIFFICULTY IN SEEKING OUT SUPPORT FOR MENTAL HEALTH ISSUES IS THE FEAR OF BEING MISUNDERSTOOD BY PARENTS.

Parents dont know everything, (despite what they think) but they love you.

Your parent, grandparent, siblings, or caregivers only want what is best for you. Sometimes the only way they know how to help is by letting you figure it out on your own. More than anything they want you to be safe and happy. It can be jarring for a parent when their kid tells them that they're unhappy and need help, and the truth is that they probably don't know what to do either. If this is true for your parents (grandparents, siblings, etc.) then you should just be honest. If they can't help you, ask them to find someone who can. If your parent doesn't offer any support, reach out to someone else. Teachers and school counselors are there to help and they care. You can ALWAYS find someone who cares to help!

We live in a time where information and millions of people are simply at our fingertips. If you need to find someone to talk to, or just people who are going through similar things, the internet can be a powerful tool. Social media can serve as a tool to meet people via group chats, forums, or being active on mental health accounts. There are also black influencers (like Demetrius Harmon) who use their platforms discuss mental health issues. You can follow hashtags, such as #blackboyjoy and #blackgirlmagic, to find encouragement in your community.

hey! just checking in to make sure you've been doing okay!

hi. i'm really glad that you texted me because i haven't been doing my best lately. come over for a movie?

there in 20 with popcorn.

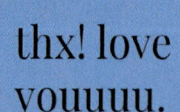

thx! love youuuu.

Chapter 6

Highs + Lows

As much as people tell you, "Just wait, it will get better," it's not always that simple. There may be times that you feel like nothing can make things better--and that's okay. All you can do is control how you react to those feelings. It's sort of like a roller coaster. Some days you'll be up, and others you'll come crashing down. Every now and then you get a fun little loop, but it's worth it for the exhilaration at the end.

The most important advice I can give is:

THERAPY THERAPY THERAPY

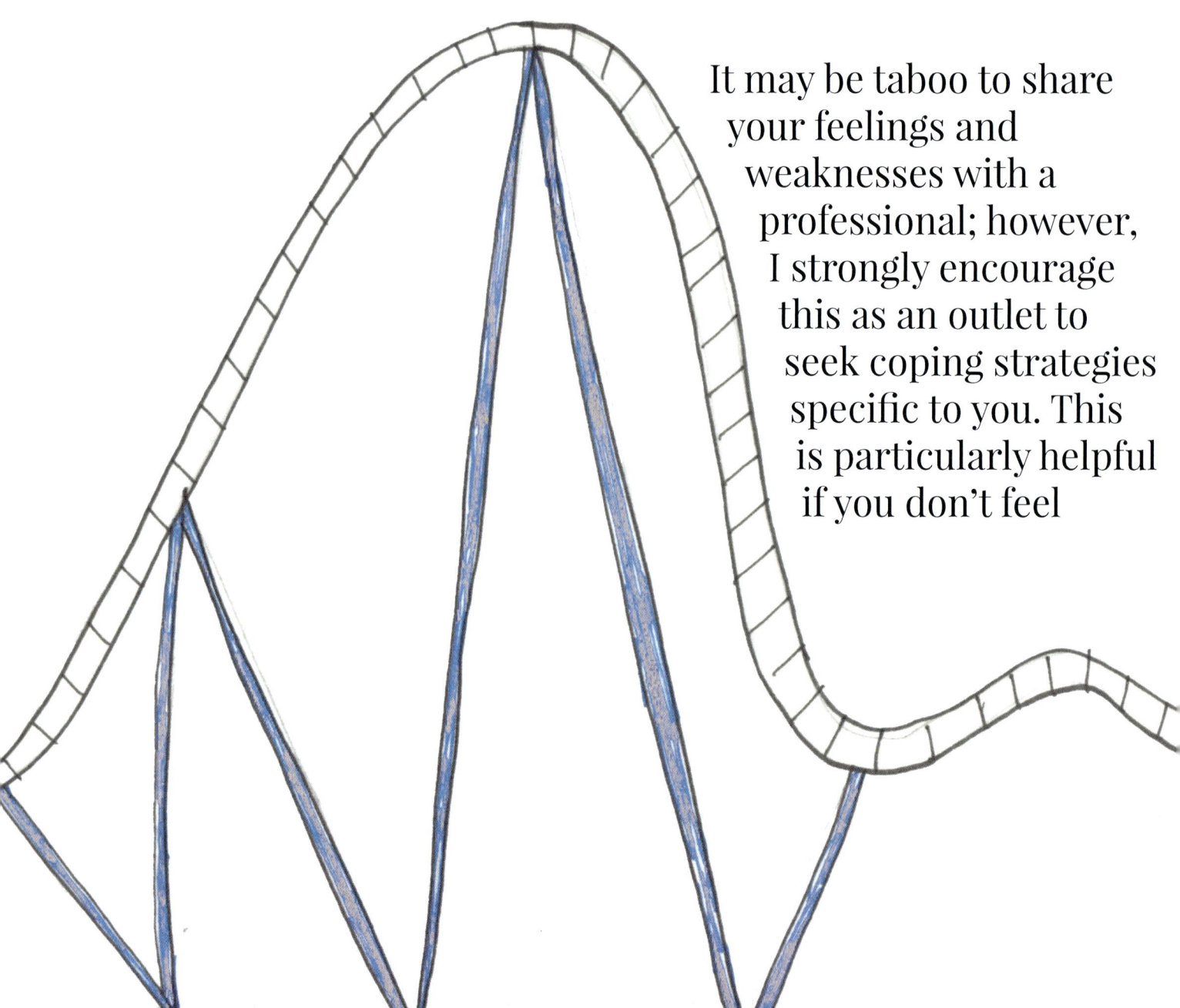

It may be taboo to share your feelings and weaknesses with a professional; however, I strongly encourage this as an outlet to seek coping strategies specific to you. This is particularly helpful if you don't feel comfortable talking to your parents. Finding a therapist can be a bit like choosing a new friend.

Your therapist should make you feel comfortable. Whatever you are looking to get out of therapy, your therapist should have knowledge of that. They should understand your goals and why you decided to seek out help. More than anything your therapist should adapt to your form of communication. If you prefer to have someone listen to you talk for an hour you should find a therapist that works that way. If you want someone to lecture to you, find that kind therapist.

THERAPY CAN BE A HELPFUL TOOL TO LEARN ABOUT YOURSELF AND EXPRESS YOURSELF.

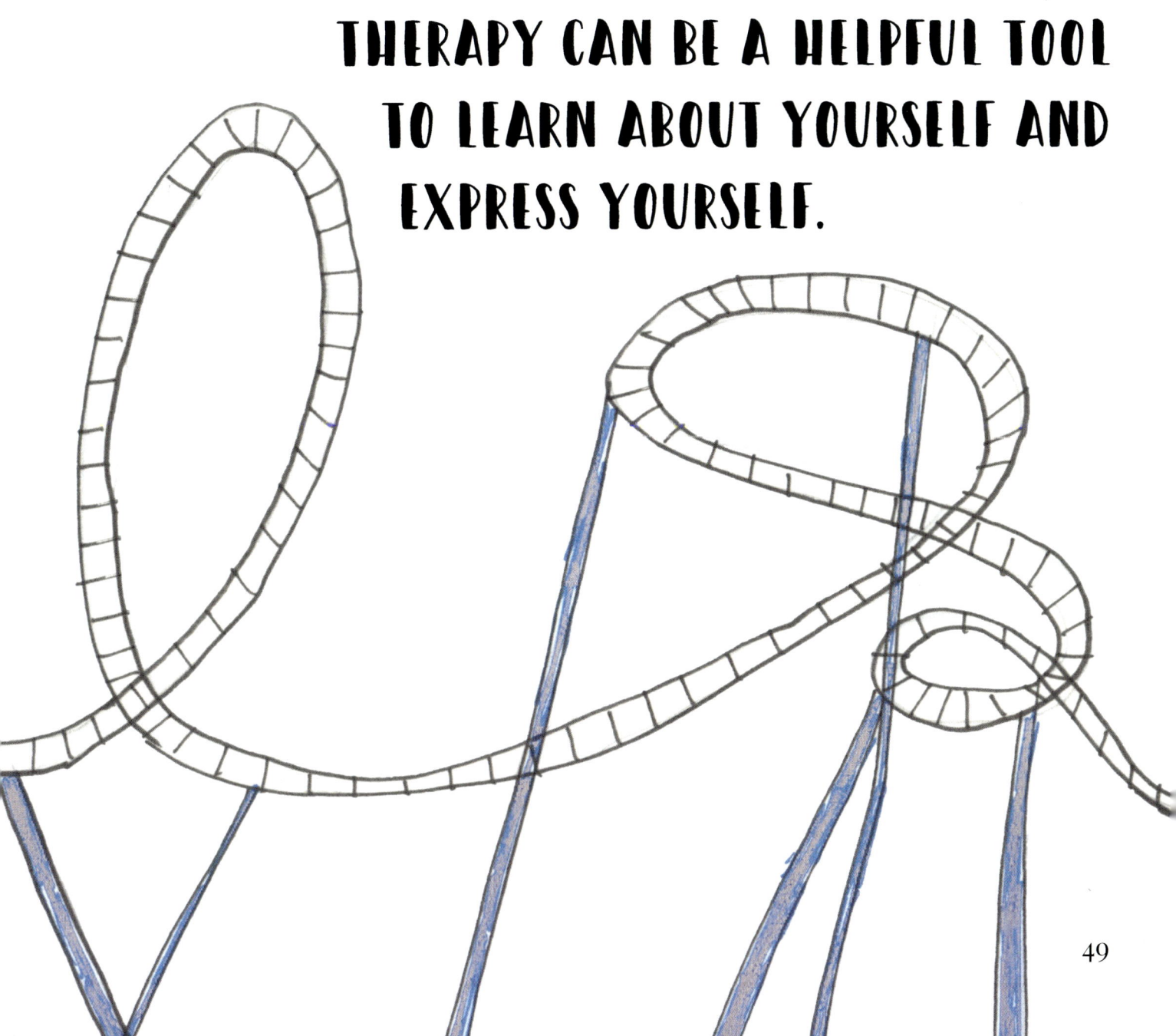

ME!

So, why did I care to spend 2 years reading, writing and drawing for this book? I have dealt with anxiety for most of my life, usually manifesting in social awkwardness and the occasional panic attack. In my junior year of high school, I lost one of my closest friends and I fell into a depression that permanently has affected my life.

My mom had to hold me in bed when I woke up with an anxiety attack, and I stopped talking to my friends. After months of isolation and seeing a therapist with every ounce of my old self drained, I slowly began to feel myself again. While recovering, I noticed how much stronger I was having gone through the tribulations of my junior year.

I wanted to write a book in part to share with others what I wish I had known when I began this project, but also to have something to come back to the next time I need guidance.

I feel a unique aspect of me writing this book rather than an adult or professional is that I come from the perspective of a black teenager who has gone through what I am writing about. I believe this is what makes this book powerful—I am a part of the group I am bringing a voice to.

THIS IS FOR US.